Albert L Swope

Growing Lemon Balm

A Home Gardener's Guide

By Albert L. Swope

Albert L Swope

Copyright

© Copyright 2019 Albert L. Swope

All Rights Reserved.

ISBN: 9781798466162

Albert L Swope

Disclaimer

No warranty whatsoever is being expressed or implied regarding the contents of this book.

Albert L Swope

Also Published By This Author

- Lemongrass: A Home Gardener's Guide
- The Bean: A Home Gardener's Guide
- The Chili Pepper: A Home Gardener's Guide
- Growing Sweet Marjoram: A Home Gardener's Guide
- Tarragon: A Home Gardener's Guide

Albert L Swope

Table of Contents

Introduction

Tools Required

Growing Lemon Balm

Tips for Growing Lemon Balm

How to store lemon balm

Conclusion

Albert L Swope

Introduction

Lemon Balm (Melissa officinalis) is mint and can be used for a variety of oils, bath salts, and tinctures. It is not as well-known as an herbal remedy plant as some of the others, particularly, peppermint. However, learning how to grow lemon balm can be of immense help to you.

The lemon balm plant is known as Melissa officinalis. It is a perennial herb that grows short, but full. It has a lemon scent, and if you allow it, the plant will develop small white flowers.

Like the peppermint and spearmint plants, you want the leaves and not the flowers. Take care with the lemon plant because the herb can be invasive and overtake other plants in your garden. The seeds are able to grow well, and other plants can be overly invaded by them. As an invasive plant, you want to keep it from flowering, so more seeds do not spread.

Besides being used in bath salts and oils, lemon balm is great in tea and potpourris. For aromatherapy, you can extract the oils from the leaves and use the oil in a diffuser or as part of a bath. You can also steep the leaves in water for ten minutes to produce tea. Another interesting property of lemon balm is the scent it gives off because we find it pleasing but insects are repelled by it. Many of the plants and herbs have a natural defense against certain insects to protect the growth of the leaves and flowers.

Now that you know why you want to grow the plant, it is time to learn how you can grow it. You will gain knowledge of what kind of tools to use in growing the plant, plus:

- How to grow it in your vegetable garden;
- How to grow it in pots;
- How to grow it indoors.

In the end, there are a few tips to help you grow your lemon balm plant with success.

Albert L Swope

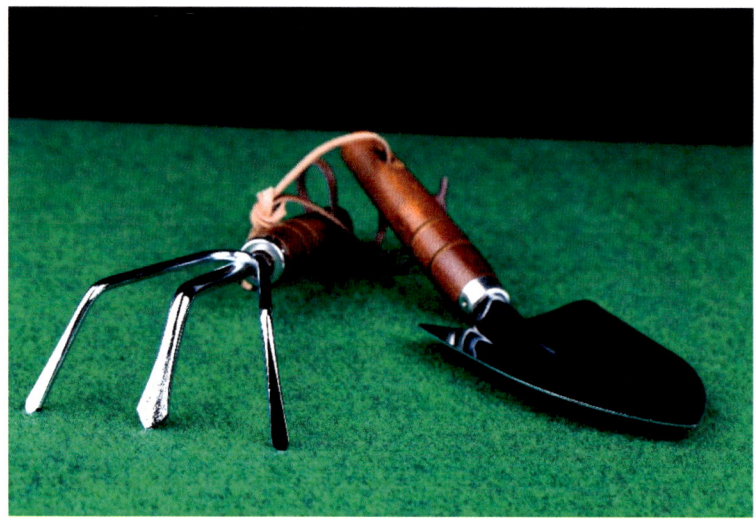

Tools Required

Before you can start to plant lemon balm, you need to understand the type of plant you are dealing with and get the tools you need. There are three methods to growing lemon balm that is discussed in more detail later. The valuable tool discussion comes before how to plant to ensure you have the knowledge and materials to be ready.

You must make a decision as to whether you are going to grow your plant in a garden, pot, or indoors. Key determinations come from the temperature, sun, and the water your plant requires. It also comes down to what other plants you may already grow and space you have.

It was mentioned in the introduction that lemon balm seeds could be invasive. New plants can grow quickly and overtake a garden. Due to the invasive qualities of the plant, you may want to have a separate area in your garden that is protected from your other plants.

If you live in a zone that is not friendly to lemon balm, you may need to raise your plant indoors.

Find the guide of information in this book that tells you the zone, temperature, and moisture to determine if you will garden inside or out, and in containers or the ground.

Gear Needed
To begin, you will need some gardening gear.

- Gloves
- Spade
- Organic soil meant for mint plants, often an orchid soil that allows for water to move quickly through the container or ground to prevent root rot.
- Fish emulsion
- Water container or hose
- Containers

If you are going to plant your lemon balm into the ground, you do not have to worry about containers. You can also put them in raised beds outside. The same principles will apply. You need to focus on the amount of water, the type of soil, and ensure the plant is going to receive the proper amount of sun at the correct temperatures to ensure success.

Your containers do not need to be more than a half-gallon in size for one plant. You can also grow the plants in a raised bed as long as there are 18 inches between each plant.

Speak with your local garden store regarding the seeds and soil to ensure you have the proper pH and type of soil for the seeds to grow.

You can also start with a cutting from a grown lemon balm plant. Starting with a cutting means new roots need to form and become rooted in the soil versus starting from a seed that will take 6 to 8 weeks to appear above ground, and possibly a couple more weeks before the seedlings are strong enough to be firmly planted in the pot or container you are going to use.

Growing Lemon Balm

Growing any plant requires the knowledge of where it grows best, how it grows well, and when to begin your plantings. Lemon balm is one of the easiest plants to grow if you know what you are doing.

It grows best in a cool season, with sun or part-shaded. It is also considered a hardy plant that can be in zone 5 and above. For those who do not know, there are zones the plant community goes by to tell you where and how well a plant will grow. The zones were created by the USDA for hardiness, and there are 11 different zones. If you want to know more about zone maps, you can find them quite easily. The zones tell you whether something is cool or warm. Zone 5 is a middle of the USA growing zone, where temperatures are relatively cool, even in summer you have lower temperatures than in the southern regions, but it can be warmer than the upper states. Alaska even has a few zones 5 areas in the southeast.

If you are going to grow your plant outdoors, but live in a zone 5 area, it is best to begin your seedlings inside. You should do this 6 to 8 weeks prior to the "last" frost. "Last" is subjective because in many zones 5 areas, frost can happen in May and June. You need to monitor the temperature and weather of your area. However, you should be able to transplant your growing plants in late March or mid-April depending on the current weather and where you live.

The Starter Pot

If you are going to transplant lemon balm into your outdoor vegetable garden, you need a starter pot. You can use little seed starters, where you barely cover the tiny seeds. Use potting soil or compost that you have. Watering should be a minimum. Keep the soil around the lemon balm from drying out, but do not soak it. Germination takes 10 to 14 days. After you see seedlings that are strong, you can transplant your lemon balm.

In the Vegetable Garden

Transplanting your lemon balm requires a spacing of 18 inches. Each plant that has grown from the seed and is strong enough to plant should be removed from the starter pot, and spaced accordingly. Make sure to bury the roots. You do not have to dig a deep hole, just make sure the soil surrounds the plant to give it stability and to let the roots take hold in the ground.

When choosing a place in your vegetable garden, you want a partially shady spot. The plants need to be safe from the high noon sun. Lemon balm also requires a fertile soil that is moist, but not soaked. The plants that are in partial sun, with moist soil will become more succulent than those left exposed in the sun.

In Pots

If you have chosen to create your lemon balm for pots, then you can directly plant the seeds in the pot of your choice. You want to have a pot that you can move, so it is in part sun, but also one that is well draining. The soil you use in the pot should be pH 6 or 7, where you have a soil that drains the water. Perlite with an organic potting soil is often the best for nutrition of mint roots. Remember that, in a pot, you are not gathering nutrients from the ground, which means you need to use a soil that can sustain the roots and one that will accept fish emulsion when necessary. Lemon balm can be in a small container unless you decide to grow more than one plant in the pot. A half-gallon pot is enough.

You do need to prune the plant, ensure it does not flower, and add fish emulsion after three months from when you planted the seeds. You can keep the plant growing year-round, with the proper nutrients in the soil.

Once the lemon balm seeds begin to sprout it is imperative that you thin the plants. You want to keep one or more plants growing 18 inches apart. If you have a small pot, keep only one plant going. Choose the hardiest.

Indoors
Growing lemon balm indoors is essentially growing the plant in pots. However, the lighting and amount of water used is where things will differ. You want a pot that you can either be placed by the window in partial sun or one you can move as the sun changes. If you are growing in

your home in a room that does not have much sun, then grow lamps are necessary. You should never have a lamp pointed directly at the plant. Instead, provide partial shade and turn the lamps off at night.

You do need the temperature to mirror the outdoors, and since the plant likes "cool" weather, you do not want it to reach over 65 degrees Fahrenheit often. You should grow lemon balm with similar plants for temperature and sun exposure unless you have multiple rooms for the plants.

In a greenhouse, you will need to regulate the temperature to fit the plants you are growing, which means like temperature plants.

Albert L Swope

Tips for Growing Lemon Balm

Growing lemon balm with success is about ensuring you have the proper containers, temperature, water, and conditions. You have learned about growing. Now you need the tips that will ensure your success. Lemon balm is a perennial, which means it flowers and grows each year. As long as frost does not kill the roots of the plant, you have a long-lasting growth, where you can harvest the leaves as you need them.

Here are some tips for growing lemon balm and harvesting it with success.

- You will want to check the soil for moisture. There is no set watering regime to follow. Soggy soil that does not drain well causes root rot. Therefore, if the topsoil is dry, without moistness, you need to water

the plant. Containers should be given minimal water, and you may want to get on a cycle where you water each day.
- Brown leaves can be a sign of a lack of moisture. You will need to adjust by watering more.
- Brown leaves can also occur in temperatures that are too high or in too much sun. Eliminate these options if you find the soil is moist.
- Lemon balm can be grown successfully in temperatures between 50- and 70-degrees F but is best at 65 degrees F.
- Fish emulsion for ground plants should be added every two weeks.
- For container and indoor plants, use fish emulsion once every six to eight weeks. Do not overwater when giving the emulsion.
- For best accuracy, test the soil pH and examine the leaves of the plant. A healthy plant will continue to grow, sprout new leaves, and offer green leaves, with a nice fragrance. Help is needed if the leaves turn, fall off, or if the plant growth is stunted.
- When you harvest the plant, do not take more than 25 percent of the plant's leaves at a time. It takes a lot for new growth, which means you jeopardize the plant if you take too many leaves.
- Not all insects are repelled by the plant. Aphids and mealy bugs can create issues. If you see insects on your plant, you should address it with an organic and non-harmful repellent. The earlier you detect problems and treat them, the quicker you can resolve it.
- When you remove the leaves, you do not want to leave them to dry in the sun. They will oxidize quickly, losing some of the healthful properties and fragrance. They should be used immediately for infusions. If you use them for tea, dry the leaves in a

- cool place that will not create oxidation. Some oxidation will occur, but not like in the sun.
- You should not have to repot your plant as long as you continue to remove leaves and flowers. New growth is fine, but also make sure you manage it while providing proper nutrients.

If you have more questions, please seek advice from your local Master Gardener or Horticultural Specialist near you. The key to growing lemon balm with success is ensuring shade is offered, cool temperatures without dipping into frost periods, and enough moisture to feed the plant without creating root rot.

Consistency is key to successful planting, with any flower, plant or tree. As long as you keep to a proper routine for watering, nutrients, and sunlight, your lemon balm will grow and produce fragrant leaves for a variety of health-related needs.

How to store lemon balm

The beauty of lemon balm is that it can be used and stored in a variety of ways. To store your lemon balm, you have essentially three options:

- For short-term storage, you can either store it fresh in the refrigerator,
- For long-term storage you can:
    - freeze the fresh herbs for later use, which can be accomplished in more than one way,
    - or dry the herbs and store in your cupboard, pantry or root cellar.

How to dry lemon balm

First, head to your garden with a sharp pair of herb scissors. Gather a large handful of tender green shoots with your left hand and cut them with your right, making sure the cut ends of the stems all lineup.

Next, give the handful of lemon balm a few quick, brisk shakes to dislodge any insects and debris, then bind the base of the stems with a rubber band. Continue this process until you have up to six or seven bunches. You can't miss having a sizable amount of lemon balm in the winter. Make sure you harvest enough bunches, so you don't run out of homegrown herbs.

Once the bunches are inside, unfold one paperclip for each bunch and use the paperclip's "S" as a hook, sliding one end under the rubber band and using the other end to hook the bunch of lemon balm to its drying location. You could extend a piece of jute twine from one side of your kitchen window to the other, fastening it securely to a teacup hook installed on each end of the window frame. Then hang the bunches up on the twine, placing them a good five or six inches apart to allow for good air circulation.

The same drying line can also serve to dry thyme, basil, parsley, and other herbs later in the season. Your dried lemon balm is ready in four to six weeks; sometimes sooner if the weather isn't overly humid. Once they're fully dried, cut off the rubber band, separate the dried sprigs, and crush the leaves. Proceed to store the crushed lemon balm in a Mason jar in a dark cupboard.

How to store your lemon balm inside the refrigerator

The refrigerator can be used for short-term storage of fresh lemon balm. To refrigerate lemon balm:

- ➢ Wash and lightly pat dry.
- ➢ Wrap in a paper towel.
- ➢ And seal in a plastic bag; then put the crisper drawer in the refrigerator inside the fridge.

How long does fresh lemon balm last in the refrigerator?

If properly stored, fresh lemon balm will usually keep well for about 10 to 14 days in the refrigerator.

How to freeze lemon balm

Cookie Sheet method

Frozen is, perhaps, the second best method for using lemon balm and optimizing the flavor of the herb. To freeze lemon balm:

- ➢ Remove the leaves from the stem
- ➢ Put the leaves on a parchment paper lined cookie sheet in successive layers of parament paper and lemon balm. For best results, at most three to five layers are recommended.
- ➢ You can place a final layer of parchment paper and top with a second cookie sheet to gently press the leaves flat.
- ➢ Let the leaves freeze a few hours or overnight.
- ➢ Once the leaves are thoroughly frozen, remove the leaves from the cookie sheet and put them loosely inside small freezer bags or containers for long-term storage.

Ice Cube Method

One way of freezing Lemon balm is to add the leaves to ice cube trays in water or juice before freezing. This method is useful for adding small quantities to recipes, especially soup, stews, and casseroles.

Equipment Required:

- Salad Spinner or two clean spongy kitchen towels
- Kitchen shears or sharp knife and cutting board
- Ice Cube Trays
- measuring spoons

Ingredients:

- Entire leaf or hacked Lemon balm
- Fresh faucet water
- Pick through the fresh Lemon balm and dispose of damaged leaves. Spin drying or pat dry between two kitchen towels to remove much moisture as could reasonably expect.
- Strip off the leave from the stem.

- Either dice the Lemon balm and add to ice cube tray or add whole leaves to the ice cube trays.
- Fill every compartment with leaves.
- Top off with water or juice and place in the freezer.
- When the ice cubes have frozen, remove the lemon balm cubes.
- Store in water/air-proof freezer bag or container in your freezer.

How to use cubes:

- These Lemon balm ice cubes can be utilized in sauces and soups.
- To use the cubes as fresh herbs in salad dressings or dishes with minimal liquid, place the cube in a glass at room temperature water until it thaws and strain to remove the lemon balm from the water.

Vacuum Sealer Method

This method preserves more color and flavor by keeping the sprigs entire and sealed shut.

Equipment Required:

- Vacuum sealer with proper bag material
- Salad Spinner or clean spongy kitchen towels
- Kitchen shears or sharp knife

Method:

- Wash and gently spin dry or smear with kitchen towels to remove excess moisture.
- Cut or cut off tough woody stems and stained or harmed takes off.
- Make a bag from the moving material sufficiently large to hold the sprigs of Lemon balm and permit space between the herb and the last seal, and seal one end.
- Name bag with substance and date fixed.
- Place herb sprigs into the bag.
- Vacuum seal the bag.
- Place in the freezer level. After the bags have solidified solid, they can be put away upright, consuming up little room in the freezer.

How long can lemon balm be stored in the freezer?

If properly stored, it will maintain the best quality for about 4 to 6 months but will remain safe beyond that time.

Conclusion

As a perennial plant, you can continuously grow lemon balm indoors. If you have a set up where you use pots, you can put your plants outdoors during the spring and summer, but ensure they are growing well indoors during frost seasons. If you grow your plant in the ground, expect it to go dormant and reappear from the roots once the frost is gone.

Lemon balm is a useful herb to grow. Given its "herb" status, lemon balm is also a fairly easy plant to keep living, as long as you pay attention to the moisture level in the soil. You never want the roots to be dry, so getting into a routine with daily water to ensure the soil stays moist, but not soaking wet.

You can also allow the soil to be moist for a few days by soaking the plant or using an in-container water option that keeps the plant moist as needed. The important thing to remember is that soil does need to have water for healthy roots. It also needs proper nutrients.

Once a plant is growing and continues to create new leaves, you have to provide more nutrients, especially with container plants. After the soil nutrients are used up, your plant will need more food. Fish emulsion is considered the best.

The tips you have learned, along with the basic information on how to grow the plants will ensure you have a happy, healthy plant that offers you all of the healing properties this plant is known for. You have plenty of uses for lemon balm, including as a cleaning agent, tea, or mood enhancer.

Made in United States
Orlando, FL
03 May 2022